50 "Simple" TRUTHS FOR A COMPLEX AND COVID-19 WORLD

Volume 1

BY

REVEREND ANDREW D. SINGLETON, JR., C.P.A., M.DIV.

50 Simple Truths For A Complex And Covid-19 World
by Andrew Singleton, Jr.
ISBN-13: 978-1-947288-65-2

Printed in the United States
10 9 8 7 6 5 4 3 2 1

Cover design by: Legacy Design Inc
Legacydesigninc@gmail.com

Published by
Life To Legacy, LLC
P.O. Box 1239
Matteson, IL.
877-267-7477
www.Life2Legacy.com
Life2legacybooks@att.net

Table of Contents

INTRODUCTION

A Collection of Quotations Regarding Covid-19, Spiritual, Business and Personal Matters

Over my 40 plus years as a minister to God's people, I have invented a number of sayings, mostly from sermons, to help people in their personal and spiritual lives. I would like to think that for the most part, these are original sayings of mine; but, if not, forgive me for not giving credit where credit is due.

I am writing these sayings now because on August 4, 2021, Victory will be celebrating its 25th Anniversary of ***"Building Victorious Christlike Lives"*** in the southwest suburbs of Chicago. Since Victory is halfway to celebrating Jubilee (50 years), I wrote 50 sayings in this first volume.

Also, I am writing now because of the drastic changes brought about by the Covid-19 Pandemic and how it has made the world much more complex.

Known by my congregation as an illustrator, and some call me the "props preacher." I always seek truth first, and then try to find an illustration that will help keep the truth taught remembered. One of my personal favorites is that of a 3 to 4 piece children's puzzle, that when completed, you turn it over and something complex has been made e.g. (city, zoo) as a simple child's puzzle is being put together (see New Testament section *Witnessing Begins In the Home*). That is why I have entitled this book "Simple Truths for a Complex and Covid-19 World." These truths will be helpful in the spiritual and natural realms of life. For each simple truth, there will also be an accompanying scripture supporting the story along with illustrated spiritual application challenges to one's life. I am thankful for the quotes I used from my former pastor, the late Bishop Arthur M. Brazier, my best friend Rod Clemons, my barber Charles Freeman, and businessman Mike Lewis.

BOOK FORMAT

1) **A Simple Truth Statement**

2) **Story: Scripture Support – Illustration**

3) **Applications to One's Life**

    - Simple Application Challenges (SAC)

10 SIMPLE COVID-19 TRUTHS

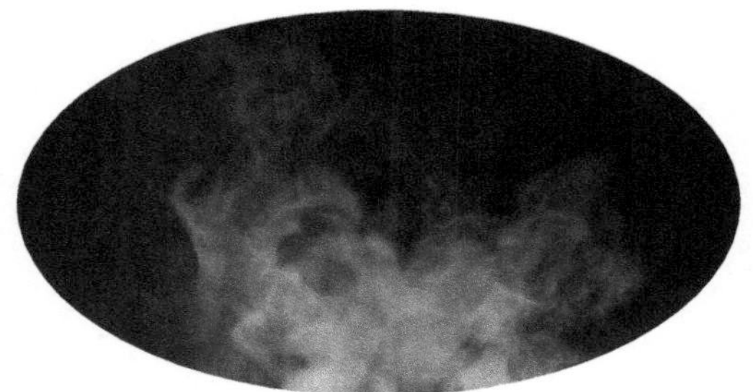

THE VAPOR CALLED LIFE

Now You See It...Now You Don't

James 4

That was the title of my first sermon after all churches were closed due to Covid-19 on March 22, 2020. James, the Lord's half-brother, was addressing Christian business folk who were acting as if they controlled tomorrow in their quest to make money. James had to teach them it is only as "the Lord wills" can we plan and do this or that (vv. 13-14).

At the beginning of 2020, no one could have known that before year's end, millions of people would have lost their lives from the Covid-19 disease. Millions of others would be sick from the disease. Untold numbers of businesses would fail, and jobs would be lost.

It is the sin of presumptuousness to think we have control over tomorrow and plan our lives as if God does not exist. One of the reasons God has permitted this Pandemic is to bring his people back to him and turn from their sinful, wicked ways (2 Chronicles 7:13-14).

The Bible teaches in Proverbs 16:3, that all of us should commit to the Lord whatever we do and he will establish our plans.

SAC

What has the Pandemic taught you regarding how fragile and temporal life is?

UNITED WE STAND, DIVIDED WE FALL

MATTHEW 12

On Wednesday, January 6, 2021, one of the most shameful moments in American history unfolded with the pro-Trump mob insurrection on our nation's Capital, instigated by former President Donald J. Trump.

Trump refused to accept the reality of his election loss and claimed without any proof, that the election was "rigged and stolen." His actions parallel with the Pharisees' inability to recognize the truth of Jesus being Israel's long-awaited Messiah; proven with the casting out of a blind and mute demon from a man in (vv. 22-28).

Hatred against Jesus blinded the Pharisees to what others could clearly see and led to their ludicrous position of saying Jesus cast out the demon by the power of Satan. However, it is impossible for Satan to cast out Satan, if so, he would be divided against himself.

If it is ludicrous for Satan's kingdom to be divided against itself, the same holds true for your household. Families living in unity before the Pandemic remained unified during the Pandemic. Unity is being able to go down the same path in life together, without falling into discord or disarray (Amos 3:3).

SAC

Can you identify a time when bitterness against someone blinded you to the truth? As it relates to your family, did the Pandemic uncover division or unity?

THREE TYPES OF PEOPLE

Takers, Fakers and Difference Makers

LUKE 10

Jesus informed an expert of the law (Scribe) that love of God and neighbors was essential for a person to obtain eternal life. Jesus tells a parable to answer the scribe's question of who is his neighbor (vs.29).

The story tells of a man as he traveled from Jerusalem to Jericho. His life now impacted by three classes of people whom I call the takers, fakers and difference makers (vv.30-37).

The **takers** rob the man, beat him, and leave him for dead. The **fakers** were the priests and Levites; religious people probably coming from temple worship who did nothing to help the dying man.

The difference maker was a Samaritan who was viewed as being an outsider to God's covenant people. However, he alone helped the injured man, bandaged his wounds and took him to an inn to be taken care of at his own expense.

Difference makers see everyone as their neighbor irrespective of race, color or creed. Millions of people were difference makers during the Pandemic.

SAC

In what ways were you a difference maker to others during the Pandemic?

IF YOU ONLY USE YOUR REAR VIEW MIRROR

You Will Have An Accident

PHILIPPIANS 3

Paul issues a call for us to stop living in the past when he states, "forgetting the things which are behind" (v.13). However, as human beings, we have no ability to forget the past. What Paul is teaching us is not to allow past failures, disappointments, troubles, and even success, to keep us from moving forward in life.

The year 2020 was clearly the year of the entire world in turmoil due to the Covid-19 Pandemic. Millions sick, hundreds of thousands dead, businesses failing, jobs lost, and loss of physical contact with others.

As more and more people are vaccinated, we must not let all of the turmoil of 2020 keep us from moving forward. In 2021, as believers, Paul encourages us to "keep our eye on the prize and press forward to the high calling of God that is in Christ Jesus" (vs.14).

SAC

Is the trauma from Covid-19 inhibiting you from moving forward in 2021? If yes, how will you overcome it?

IF GOD PERMITS IT, YOU CAN TAKE IT!

1 CORINTHIANS 10

Paul makes it clear that believers can rely on God's faithfulness when he permits tests and trials in our lives (v. 13). If God permits it, then there's a purpose for it. For example, God permitted Satan to test Job. The purpose of the trial was to prove God to be worthy of worship based on who he is, as opposed to all that he had given Job.

Like an egg, God knows we are fragile. Therefore, he will never put more on us than we can endure. If God permits it, he always provides the way of escape. Ironically, the way out of a test is by going through it, not around it. In Daniel 3:19-28, King Nebuchadnezzar of Babylon threw the three Hebrew boys into a fiery furnace. However, God got the glory because he intervened in the fire. In the end, the three Hebrew boys emerged untouched by the flames without even the smell of smoke. Trust God in the trial because he will see you through.

SAC

Name at least three tests and trials that God took you through when your prayer was for God to keep you out of the test or trials, especially during Covid-19.

PEACE OR WORRY

THE CHOICE IS YOURS

MARK 4

While Jesus was in the boat with his disciples, a terrible storm arose on the Sea of Galilee. The disciples were terrified. After seeing the Sea of Galilee on a trip to the Holy Land in 2018, along with over 100 believers from Victory and Lighthouse Church of All Nations and their Pastor Dan Willis, I can understand why the sudden storms arise. With mountains on either side of the sea, violent winds have no way to escape, creating a funnel effect. The disciples panicked as water filled the boat. But Jesus is sleeping, because he knew his Father was watching over him (vv. 36-41).

As Jesus spoke peace to the stormy sea, so can He calm the turbulence of a Corona Virus World that has brought waves of despair into the lives of many believers. Yes, there is a God-given peace that passes all understanding for the believer (Philippians 4:6-7). Like Jesus, one of the ways we know we have this peace is by observing our daily sleep pattern. The Bible says, "he gives his beloved sleep" (Ps.127:2). Sleeping well is a good sign that a person is not overwhelmed with worry.

SAC

Rate your daily sleep on a scale of 1 to 10 with 10 being very good.

WHEN FAITH TRUMPS FEAR

I SAMUEL 17

January 20, 2021, was the Inaugural Ceremony for the 46th President of the United States, Joseph R. Biden and the first female Vice President of the United States, Kamala Harris.

History was also made on January 13, 2021 with the second impeachment of now former President Donald Trump. His presidency was marked by the Goliaths of fear, hate, racism, injustice and denying the seriousness of the Covid-19 Pandemic from the beginning.

In this text, Israel cowered in fear when faced with their enemy's Philistine champion warrior named Goliath. None of the Israelites, except young David, dared to fight him (vv. 8-11). Israel needed "no Goliath" like we needed a "no Trump" to move forward as a nation. Those that play the card game called Bid Whist know that a no trump requires the most skill to play. As we move into the Biden/Harris era, we must have confidence that a little faith can overcome objects of great fear and that we can move past the damage done to our country during the Trump administration.

Just as surely as David defeated the giant Goliath with a small stone, we will defeat the aforementioned Goliaths of our time.

SAC

What problems in your life are you letting fear stop you from getting the victory? Remember to get the "victory" it is not by power, or by might, it is by the Spirit of the living God (Zechariah 4:6).

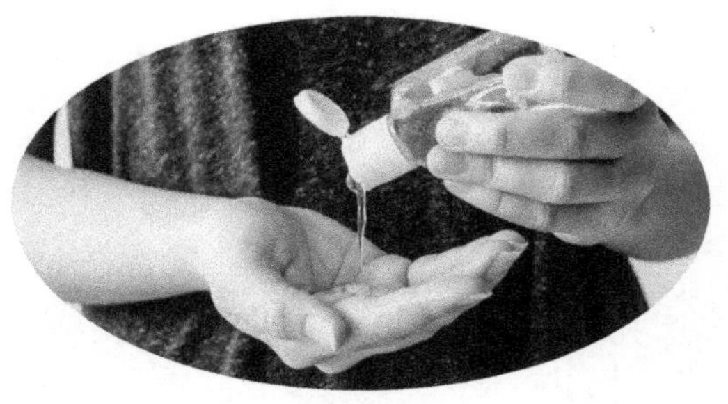

THE SANCTIFIER IS THE SPIRITUAL SANITIZER

1 JOHN 1

One of the unforgettable memories from the Covid-19 Pandemic was the constant use of hand sanitizer to help prevent the spread of the Corona Virus. Sanitizers clean our hands outwardly, but God pours out his Holy Spirit, who is called the Sanctifier, and cleans the believer inwardly.

The Holy Spirit sets believers apart by continually cleansing them from the inside by the shed blood of Jesus Christ (vv. 5-10).

SAC

How has knowing God set you apart as his child affected your everyday life?

LIVE YOUR LIFE

One Day At A Time

MATTHEW 6

The Covid-19 Pandemic caused a lot of worrying for millions of people. Physical and financial health problems caused even some believers to be unduly anxious or over concerned … the very definition of worry. I often say worry is concern on steroids.

In verses 25-34, Jesus connects worrying about the life essentials to what we shall eat, drink, and wear. Jesus knew the day-to-day testimony of so many people was "hurry, worry, bury." The illustration of God feeding birds in these verses has a very special application to me. After being unemployed for two years (1978-1980), I became very discouraged. I was having difficulty paying my mortgage. I had a wife and a young child to support and our only car at that time had been repossessed. As I sat on my mother's porch having a pity party, suddenly a bird flew down, grabbed a worm and hopped toward me with the worm in his mouth. An eternity seemed to pass as the Lord convicted me of my lack of trust in him to supply my needs. From that day forward, I have tried to live my life one day at a time.

The same God who was taking care of my yesterday, will also be in my tomorrow.

SAC

Can you remember a time during the Pandemic when your lack of trust in God made you ashamed and caused you to trust Him more in the future?

ONLY THE STRONG SURVIVE

and Their Strength is in the Lord

ISAIAH 40

As many of you know, the Corona Virus has been particularly deadly to the elderly, the weak, and those with underlying health conditions. In the United States alone, over 20,000,000 people have tested positive and over 500,000 people have succumbed to the virus. These staggering numbers also indicate a disparity in the health care system, which makes medical care unaffordable for many African American and other people of color.

The Prophet Isaiah speaks to comfort the Israelites coming out of 70 years of captivity to the Babylonians around 536 B.C. The Hebrew word for comfort means *to breathe again*. The vaccines being administered to people all over the world are allowing people to breathe again, hopefully without wearing masks. Israel's captivity and our Pandemic taught us that even the youth get tired and want to quit. The year 2020 was a year of online schooling, quarantines, no graduations, proms, weddings, etc.

But as the Prophet Isaiah states, the believers' power source is inexhaustible because it is not in self, but the Lord (vv. 27-31). My wife loves the fact that we purchased an in-house generator. When storms cause power outages in our community, our power stays on.

P.S., my wife said I was a genius when I purchased the generator. However, the generator turns on only when the power from the electric company goes out. So it is with our relationship with God. His strength will always be turned on when we have no strength left.

SAC

Can you testify that during Covid-19 without the power of God in your life you would not have made it? Give God the glory, He truly deserves it!

10 SIMPLE SPIRITUAL TRUTHS FROM THE OLD TESTAMENT

YOU WILL NEVER GET MORE LIVING OUTSIDE OF GOD'S WILL THAN IN HIS WILL FOR YOUR LIFE

GENESIS 3

The book of Genesis teaches us that God created the entire universe to bring him glory. Only Adam and Eve were said to be made in God's likeness and image and, as a result, possessed intellect, emotion and free will. Freely, they disobeyed God's will to not eat of the Tree of the Knowledge of Good and Evil.

Adam wanted to be independent from God and Eve foolishly thought God was holding something back from them since the fruit from the tree was good for food, pleasing to the eye, and desirable for gaining wisdom (vv. 6-7)

When they ate, they became sinners, and ultimately were cast out from the Garden of Eden. They learned a person will always get less when they choose to do their will over God's will. Sin subtracts and never adds to a person's life.

In pride Adam sought to be God, in humility, God became man in the person of Jesus Christ. Every Christmas we can thank God for sending Jesus into the world, who always did God's will. This included dying on Calvary's Cross which saves the believer from Hell and reserves for them a place in Heaven.

SAC

Identify and plan to correct the areas in your life that are not in harmony with God's will for your life.

DON'T KILL THE EGYPTIAN

Bad Timing Affects God's Plans for Your Life

Exodus 2

Moses was divinely chosen to be the deliverer of God's people who were subjected to harsh labor while enslaved in Egypt. Moses, whose name means "drawn out of the water," was providentially saved from Pharaoh's decree to kill all the Hebrew boys age two and under, in order to become the deliverer of the Israelites.

However, Pharaoh's daughter pulled Moses out of the water, fell in love with him and unknowingly paid Moses' mother to raise Moses right in Pharaoh's household. At age 40, Moses became aware that he was indeed Israel's chosen deliverer, and then he killed an Egyptian who was beating an Israelite. The next day, he tried to intercede between two Israelites who were fighting. One of them said in vs. 14 "are you thinking of killing me as you killed the Egyptian?" Moses then fled for his life and 40 years went by before he began to fulfill the call upon his life to be Israel's deliverer.

Whenever you operate outside of God's timing and commissioning for your life, you will always "kill the Egyptian." That is, you will experience unnecessary suffering because you take action rather than waiting for the Lord to open doors.

SAC

Identify areas in your life that you are experiencing suffering due to not waiting on the Lord and how you plan to be more patient in the future.

FACTS ARE YOUR FRIEND WHEN FACED
With Overwhelming Challenges

EXODUS 14

After being set free from slavery, the Children of Israel once again find themselves in a perilous predicament. Pharaoh had a change of heart and sent his army to destroy Israel. With mountains on each side, Pharaoh's army behind them and a 100-foot deep Red Sea before them, the Israelites appeared to be hopelessly hemmed in.

Facts are always our friend because they precisely inform us what we need to have faith for and pray on. This passage gives the minute details concerning the size of Pharaoh's army (vv. 5-9). When we have facts, it gives us a basis to gauge how awesome God's actions are. So, God tells Moses to "stand still and by faith see the salvation of the Lord" (vv.13-14). As most of you know, the Red Sea opened up, the Israelites crossed over safely, and the Red Sea closed and destroyed Pharaoh's army.

SAC

The next time you are faced with overwhelming challenges, get the victory by "Faithing the Facts."

DON'T FAIL AT THE FINISH LINE

The Tension Between Facts and Faith

NUMBERS 13

God had used Moses to set the Israelites free from 400 years of slavery to the Egyptians. As they prepared to enter the Promised Land of Canaan, Moses sent out 12 leaders (one from each tribe) to spy out the land. When they returned, they all agreed the land was as God promised; a land flowing with milk and honey; but the facts of giants in the land caused 10 of the 12 spies to say they could not take the land because of lack of faith in the promises of God (vv. 26-33).

Both faith and facts are important when faced with a dilemma. This is the tension between the two. If you apply only faith, you will see the facts do not go away. If you apply only facts, you limit what God can do.

The Israelites' unbelief resulted in God punishing them to wander in the wilderness for 40 years. What a tragedy! After all of the miracles God performed in delivering them, they failed at the finish line.

This story has a very personal application to my life. In 2008, we were faced with a two-million-dollar shortfall in building our new church in Matteson, Illinois. Being a Certified Public Accountant, I first picked up a pencil to try to figure out what to do. The Holy

Spirit spoke to me to first go and pray (faith), then figure out what to do (facts). That resolved the tension between faith and facts as we entered our new facility in 2009 and are on track to have it fully paid off in 2026.

SAC

Identify a difficult situation when you had to resolve the tension between facts and faith. Were you successful? If not, what did you learn?

GIFTS – DISCIPLINE = DISASTER

JUDGES 13

The story of Samson is to me, one of the saddest ones in the Bible. God raised up Samson as a deliverer of Israel during the period of the Judges. He was consecrated to God as a child and given supernatural strength (vv. 2-7; 14:5-7).

But Samson lacked personal discipline and did not keep his Nazarite vow obligations. As a result, he eventually lost his strength when he was deceived by Delilah (Judges 16:1-22), and was blinded by his enemy the Philistines.

Yes, like many men, Samson was a *he-man* with a *she-weakness.* Those with great gifts from God must remember that "to whom much is given, much is required"(Luke 12:48).

SAC

Would you rate yourself as a disciplined or non-disciplined person? What have you achieved or not achieved as a result of your level of personal discipline?

WHEN THE TOUGH DECISION IS
The Right Decision

ESTHER 4

In the book of Esther, some of the Jews are still in Persia around 450 B.C. Esther, a Jew is made Queen when the former Queen Vashti was despised by King Xerxes for refusing to attend a party. One of the King's officials named Haman hated Mordecai, Esther's uncle, because Mordecai refused to bow down before him. In anger, Haman persuades the King to approve having all of the Jews in Persia killed. When Mordecai hears of this evil plot, he asks Esther to intervene, which she initially refused to do for fear the King would kill her. According to Persian law, it was unlawful to appear before the king without a request to do so.

Eventually Esther understands the lives of all the Jews in Persia are in her hands. So, she makes the tough but right decision to appear before the King who grants her favor to appear before him and is apprised of Haman's evil motives. In the end, Haman was hanged on the gallows and the edict to kill all of the Jews was reversed. Esther learned that sometimes the places and times we are in is for such a time as this (vv. 12-14).

I have always found that making tough decisions is easier when I place the welfare and needs of others above my own. When caught between a rock and a hard place, reach for the rock that is higher than you, Jesus Christ, who will give you the wisdom and courage to do the right thing, no matter how difficult it is to do so.

SAC

Identify a time when the tough decision was the right decision and what was the outcome of that decision?

YOU HAVE TO COME CLEAN

Before You Can Get Clean

PSALM 51

The 51st Psalm was written by King David after he admits to both adultery and being an accessory to murder. David had gotten Uriah the Hittite's wife pregnant, and then had her husband killed to cover up his sins. In 2 Samuel, Chapters 11-12 you can find the account where Nathan the prophet confronts David with his sin. David had to be confronted with his sins because no king (leader) can rule righteously when they themselves are unrighteous (dirty). At this point in his life David was as dirty as "Pig Pen" in the Charlie Brown stories.

David proves himself to be "the man after God's own heart" (Acts 13:22), when he confesses his sins in Psalm 51. Though he wronged both Bathsheba and Uriah, ultimately all sin is against God. You see, confession is good for the soul because it cleanses the soul (Psalm 103:1-4).

When the believer is cleansed from sin, then their relationship with God is restored and he or she can now worship and praise God in the beauty of holiness.

SAC

Since unconfessed sin affects your personal relationship with God (1 John 1:5-10), how do you use the opportunity to confess and restore your fellowship?

LORD, MAKE MY WORDS BETTER!

PROVERBS 18

Proverbs 18:21 states "The tongue has the power of life and death, and those who love it will eat its fruit." James 3:6 says "The tongue also is a fire, a world of evil among the parts of the body." The believer must get control of their tongue to be an effective witness for Christ. Our mouths that praise God should never be an instrument to curse men or use profane language (Colossians 3:8-10). The old saying "sticks and stones may break my bones, but words will never hurt me" is a falsehood. All of us have experienced spiritual, emotional, psychological and mental hurt from the fiery words of others.

You must ask yourself if your words are mostly hurting words (lying, gossiping, filthy language, angry words) or helping words (building up others, speaking wisdom, gentle, forgiving, etc.). Jesus is our example that our words should bring life and healing (Luke 4:18-22).

SAC

Name the ways in which you can make your words better on a daily basis.

TRUE LOVE WAITS BECAUSE

the Best Things in Life are Worth Waiting For

SONG OF SOLOMON 8

This book written by King Solomon tells the story of a young King Solomon who is in love with an unnamed black Shulamite woman. Today, many young people refuse to be patient and make sure their love relationships are in line with the will of God for them, and often end up living together without the benefit of a committed relationship defined by marriage (vv. 8-14).

Though the passion that Solomon and the Shulamite woman have for each is evident, the timing was not right and they waited because pleasing God was first. They understood that true love, is not something we work up, it is something the Lord sends down within us when we meet the right person at the right time. You see, "nothing beats love at first sight except love with insight".

Like the Shulamite woman loved Solomon, we believers love Jesus and are now awaiting his second coming as portrayed in Revelation 19:6-9. God is always true to his word and will return for his bride, the Church.

SAC

How have you been blessed in life when you have patiently waited for the Lord's timing?

LET JUSTICE ROLL DOWN
AMOS 5

I was a teenager during the height of the civil rights movement in the 1960's. I was a freshman at Lindbloom Technical High School in Chicago when Martin Luther King, Jr. spoke these words as a part of his immortal "I Have A Dream Speech" in 1963. "No, we are not satisfied and we will not be satisfied until justice rolls down like water, and righteousness as a mighty stream." King's quote from the book of the Prophet Amos is a judgment on Israel and a call to national repentance (vv.18-24).

We must never stop treating the poor and those who have suffered injustice fairly. Like a great river never stops flowing, we must always do what is right as waters always flow downward. Justice and righteousness flow down from our righteous just God (Psalm 67:3-4). Much progress has been made as seen in the 2008 election and 2012 re-election of our first African American President Barack Obama, and Kamala Harris as our nation's first female Vice President and woman of color in 2020.

On June 8, 2020, Victory, along with other churches and top state and local governmental officials, stood together to protest the murder of George Floyd in a "March for Justice and Love of Our Neighbor Rally."

Under our Gospel of Justice ministry at Victory, we have pledged both human and financial resources to continue the fight to end systemic racism, police brutality, white supremacy, and economic inequity in America.

SAC

What are you doing to help put an end to injustice (e.g. voting, helping the poor, protesting injustice)?

10 SIMPLE TRUTHS FROM THE NEW TESTAMENT

THE DEVIL IS A LIAR, EVEN WHEN HE'S
Telling The Truth
MATTHEW 4

After being baptized by John the Baptist and having the seal of approval to begin his public ministry by both his Father and the Holy Spirit, Jesus is then led by the Spirit into the wilderness to be tested by the Devil.

In one of three tests, Jesus is taken by the Devil to the Holy City and told to jump down from the highest point in the temple as a sign of Jesus' trust in God to keep him from harm. The Devil even quotes a part of Psalm 91:11-12, where it states God's angels will keep him from hitting the ground. In Matthew 4:7, Jesus replies "it is also written, do not put the Lord your God to the test" (Deuteronomy 6:16).

Yes, Satan told the truth when quoting from the Old Testament but not the whole truth because we must never think as believers we can do foolish things and expect God to deliver us. Bible scholars call this "the sin of presumptuousness."

Once when I was unemployed, the Devil said I had no job, and was unable to support my family. Yes, that was true, but he did not tell the whole truth that God is a provider who also in his time allowed me to get another job and support my family.

SAC

Identify at least three times that the Devil proved himself to be a liar in your personal life.

GOD'S GRACE

The Gift That Keeps On Giving

Some Bible scholars view grace, the unmerited favor of God, as the most crucial concept in Christian theology. That's because it is by God's grace that a person is brought into right relationship with Him (Ephesians 2: 8-9). This includes a person being delivered from an eternal Hell and empowered through the indwelling Holy Spirit to live their life for God after they receive forgiveness of their sins

This "saving" grace of God appeared to mankind in the person of Jesus Christ who is God in the flesh (John 1:14). Saving grace keeps on giving in this world and the world to come.

My wife and I have a 44 year-old rocking chair that all three of our children, and all seven of our grandchildren have sat in over the years. That chair has been used for two generations and may keep on going for even a third generation. God gave his one and only son over 2,000 years ago. Generation upon generation, millions upon millions of people of every race, gender, nationality and ethnicity have benefited from God's grace in sending his Son to save people from their sins when they placed their faith in him (John 3:16).

SAC

In what ways has God kept giving his grace to you and your family?

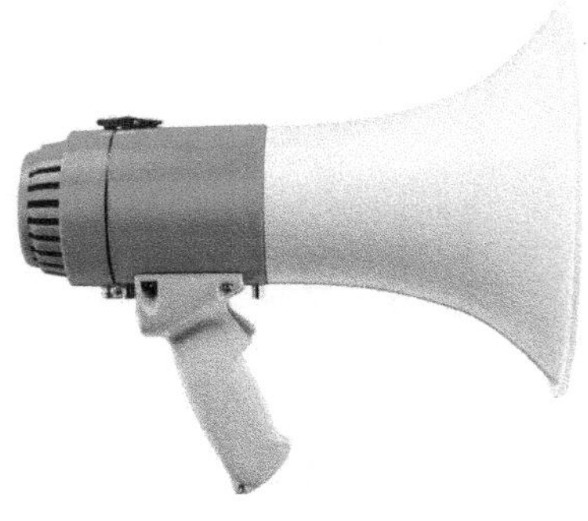

WHEN THE ONE YOU LOVE IS SICK

JOHN 11

C.S. Lewis, author and apologist said, "We can ignore even pleasure. But pain insists upon being attended to. God whispers to us in our pleasures, speaks in our conscience, but shouts in our pain. It is his megaphone to rouse a deaf world."

The Covid-19 Pandemic has been shouting for over a year for people to return to God and turn from sin and their wicked ways (2 Chronicles 7:13-15).

Countless prayers have been made for loved ones who are sick due to the Corona virus. Though we are concerned about everyone, when someone you love is sick, it becomes very personal. Lazarus, the brother of Mary and Martha and a friend of Jesus is sick in John 11. His sisters send for Jesus to come and heal Lazarus. By the time Jesus arrives, Lazarus is dead. The verse "Jesus wept" (vs. 35) is not only the shortest, but also one of the most poignant in the Bible. Even though Jesus knew he would raise Lazarus from the dead, watching his sisters grieve at his loss was almost unbearable to Jesus. We must learn to interpret a circumstance by the love of Christ and not Christ's love by the circumstance.

Jesus' grief proved "he was a man of sorrows and acquainted with grief"(Isaiah 53:1-3, KJV). Lazarus' resurrection points the believer to our own resurrection from the dead never again to experience sickness or death when Jesus returns. Only Jesus can cure the incurable disease of death (John 11:25-26).

SAC

How have you kept going when the one you love has been sick?

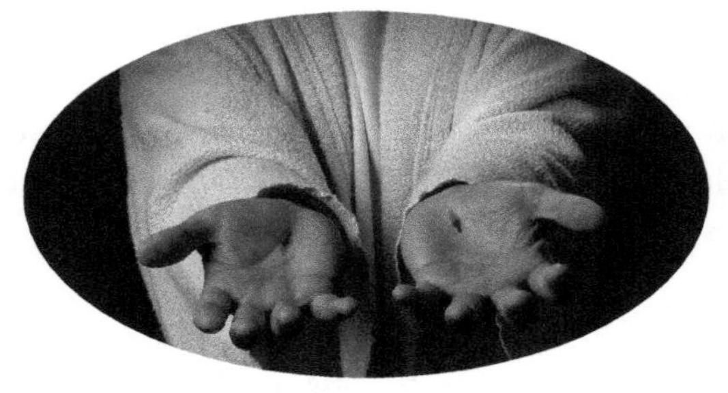

FORGIVENESS ALWAYS LEAVES SCARS

JOHN 20

After Jesus' resurrection, he met with his disciples to reinstate them, even though they had all defected from him. Thomas was not present when Jesus appeared to the other disciples, and refused to believe it was Jesus unless he saw the nail marks in Jesus' hands, put his finger where the nails were, and put his hands into his side. Jesus miraculously appears to Thomas a week later and invites him to physically touch his wounds; which Thomas refuses to do and instead worships Jesus.

Though Jesus was resurrected in a glorified body, he still had his scars, because forgiveness leaves scars (vv.19-29).

I have a clay jaguar statute in my home which was accidentally broken. Thankfully, my wife was able to repair it. Though it is still beautiful, if you look closely enough, you can still see where it was glued back together. We should be glad that Jesus forgave us at the cost of himself being scarred. One day all the redeemed will see the scars that Jesus bore on Calvary's Cross.

SAC

Identify at least one person you need to forgive and tell one person about one of your spiritual scars.

THE B.R.O.H.

The Blessings and Responsibilities of Headship

1 Corinthians 11

This was the title of a Father's Day message reflecting God's divine order of headship which is, God then Christ, then man, then woman (vv. 1-3). The head is that portion of the body that gives direction. That is why Christ is the head of the church (Ephesians 1:22).

When men submit to Christ and women to their husbands, they stand under the blessings of God and our family structures become healthy, the way God has always intended them to be. The man's headship over his wife and family is a reflection of Christ's headship over the man.

A man filled with arrogance and pride like former President Donald Trump was in my opinion, a bobblehead. However, when a man makes Christ their head, they are filled with the spirit of self-sacrifice, humility and love for their God and family. Because of that, a wife is willing to submit herself to his leadership in the family.

A true Christian man who reflects the image of his Father in heaven is blessed and handles well the responsibilities that come with headship.

SAC

Are you as a Christian man submissive to Christ; and are you as a Christian woman submissive to your husband?

TAKE YOUR THORNS TO THE THRONE OF GRACE

You Will Find God's Grace is Sufficient

2 CORINTHIANS 12; HEBREWS 4

The Apostle Paul had a sickness so severe that he prayed intently three times for God to take it away (2 Corinthians 12:1-10). God told him his grace was sufficient to take him through and that he would receive supernatural power to give him the victory over his thorns in the flesh.

Hebrews 4:16, encourages every Believer to come boldly to God's throne of grace and mercy. There, like Paul, we get what we need in the time of need.

SAC

What thorns in your life are causing you pain that you need to take to the throne of grace and leave there?

THE POWER OF THE INVISIBLE

1 TIMOTHY 1

Some things that we cannot see can have incredible power like hurricanes and tornadoes. The entire world has experienced the devastating invisible power of the Corona Virus and its related disease Covid-19. It is invisible to the naked eye, but it's devastation is visible for all to see, with millions of people sick and dead along with causing the economic collapse of many countries and businesses. Hopefully, vaccinations will continue to bring the disease under control and bring us back to some degree of normalcy.

God is also invisible, but made his power known in creating the universe, including mankind (vs.17). The invisible God indwells believers in the person of the Holy Spirit. Just as the invisible Corona virus is only seen through a microscope, our invisible God is seen only by faith (Hebrews 11:27).

The invisible God has promised to never leave the believer even at death (2 Corinthians 5: 8-9). So when the minister who does a person's committal ends with these words "ashes to ashes, dust to dust, earth to earth," we as believers must not let the decomposing body we see, take away from the reality that their invisible spirit is with their invisible God and that we will see them again when Jesus returns for his Spirit-filled church.

SAC

When has knowing that a deceased person who is with the Lord, brought comfort to you and gave you strength to keep on living your life?

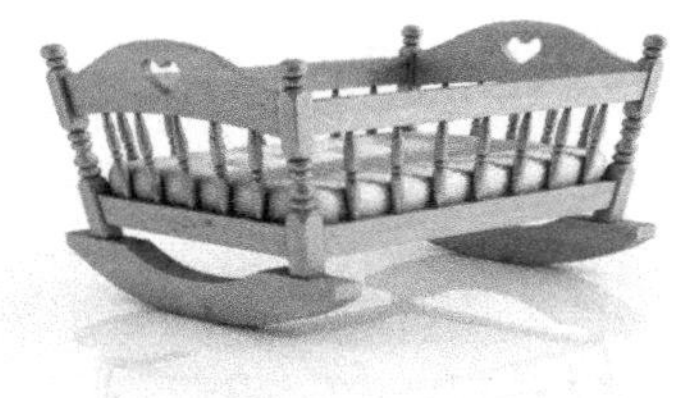

ALWAYS TAKE CARE OF YOUR MOTHER

JOHN 19

This was the title of a Mother's Day sermon. It is the third of Jesus' last sayings as He hung on the cross, and was addressed to his mother, Mary and his disciple, John. "Dear woman, here is your son and to the disciple, here is your mother" (vs. 26-27).

All throughout Jesus' ministry, he respected, validated and cared for and about women in a culture and time where women were viewed as inferior to men. Mothers bring us into the world and sometimes have to painfully watch their children leave the world before they do. A mother's influence on their children can be so strong that it has been said "the hand that rocks the cradle rules the world." It was now 33 ½ years since Mary rocked the infant Jesus. Now the wood of the cradle has transformed itself into the wood of the cross.

In the midst of Jesus' enduring the pain and humiliation of Calvary, he made sure his mother would be taken care of after he died. This duty could only be entrusted to the Disciple closest to Him, John.

SAC

It is an honor to take care of the one who took care of you. How have you shown appreciation to your mother if she is alive; and to her memory if she has passed?

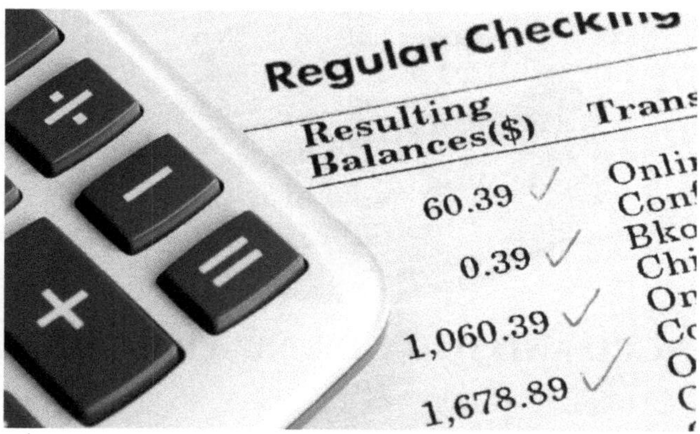

THE NEED FOR RECONCILIATION

2 CORINTHIANS 5

As believers we are new creations in Christ (v. 17), only because God reconciled us to himself through Jesus Christ. Reconciliation is the process of bringing into balance two things that must agree. For example, the balance in your check book has to be in agreement with the balance shown on your bank statement.

All of mankind was out of balance, alienated from God and reconciled by the blood of Jesus Christ (Romans 5: 6-11). Many people need to be reconciled with family members and friends so that healthy relationships can be restored. It took the blood of Jesus to reconcile mankind back to God. What does it take for you to be reconciled with a former loved one now? It could be a need for forgiveness, renewed trust, apology, repayment of monies owed, etc.

SAC

Think of at least one out of balance relationship that you have that could possibly be reconciled if you take the initiative (Matthew 5: 23-24).

CHANGED AND YOU WILL NEVER BE THE SAME

Saul, who later became the Apostle Paul, was converted to being a believer on the road to Damascus (vv. 1-6). After seeing Jesus and understanding that Jesus was truly God in the flesh, the soon to be Apostle's life was changed forever. He spent the rest of his life doing what Jesus wanted him to do. He had been born again, he had been changed.

Like Saul, I too had a supernatural encounter with Jesus on April 17, 1978. Like Saul, my life was changed for the good forever. I went from sinner to saint, from living unholy to holy, from self-controlled to God-controlled.

God gave me a new vision and purpose for life that over the years has changed and transformed me into the husband, father, son, brother, grandfather, friend, preacher, teacher, counselor, administrator and pastor he wanted me to become.

Saul, myself and millions of others know what it means to have put off the old man (sinful) and put on the new man (holy). The Bible says it is like putting on a brand new set of clothes, so much so, that any one in Christ is a new creation (2 Corinthians 5: 17).

SAC

In what ways has Jesus changed your life? Ask someone who knows you personally if they can see the change Jesus has made in your life.

10 SIMPLE BUSINESS TRUTHS

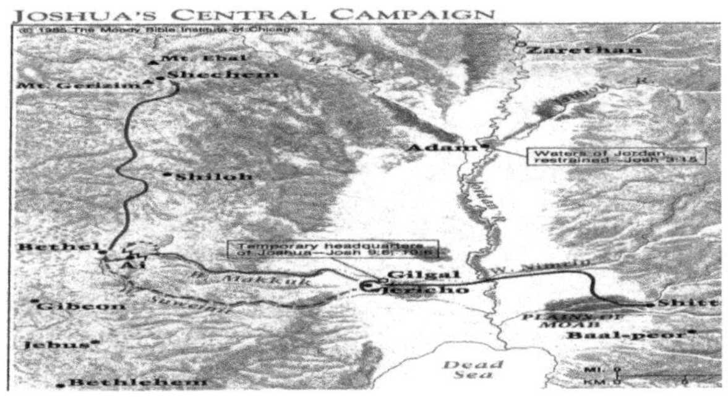

MISSION – STRATEGY= FANTASY

JOSHUA 6

The Bible says in Habakkuk 2:2-3, that a person must write the vision and make it plain before embarking on a mission or starting a business. The Bible also makes it clear in Luke 14:28-29, that a person must count the cost before starting to build lest they have insufficient funds to finish what they start. As a Certified Public Accountant (CPA) and Certified Financial Planner (CFP), I have talked to many entrepreneurial dreamers without a clear strategy or sense of timing regarding what they want to accomplish. Rarely, if ever do they succeed in their endeavors because Mission minus Strategy equals Fantasy.

As the children of Israel set out to conquer the Land of Canaan, their strategy was to divide their enemy which they did by attacking Jericho in the central area of Canaan. Doing so kept the Canaanites from uniting against them (Joshua 6:20-27).

SAC

Can you think of a time that you or someone you know experienced business or personal failure due to a lack of strategy? If you are that person, what did you learn, and were your next attempts successful?

TIMING IS EVERYTHING BECAUSE

Windows of Opportunity Close

JOHN 17

John 17 is Jesus' high priestly prayer spoken as he prepares to do his Father's will and go to Calvary's cross he said "now is the time." Jesus uses the Greek word *hora*, not *Chronos*, or watch time. Hora is the time of opportunity or occasion. There is an old Chinese saying "Opportunity has hair in the front of the head and is bald in the back."

It has been said, procrastination is the grave in which opportunity is buried.

P.S. Good timing comes from being close in relationship with God that allows you to hear His voice. God used this message to have 23 people baptized on April 3, 2011, *the most to date at Victory.*

SAC

Name a time when procrastination cost you something that should be yours or a time when you seized the opportunity and were blessed.

SOMETIMES GOOD INTENTIONS

Have Bad Outcomes

2 TIMOTHY 1

Our current facility in Matteson almost did not happen due to loan contract hold-ups with our bank in 2008. Those delays made us incur three million dollars in unreimbursed costs to our general contractor. I was to blame, because I did not want to go over the head of the bank executive responsible for finalizing our agreed upon contract. Finally, I had no choice but to meet with his superior Mr. Mike Lewis. Mr. Lewis wanted to know why he was not made aware earlier of the problem. When I gave my explanation, he responded with "That's what I call Good Intentions with Bad Outcomes." Mr. Lewis then intervened, contracts were finalized, and our general contractor received their monies.

From that incident, I learned to confront difficult situations head-on and not allow bad situations to become worse (vs. 7).

SAC

Have you ever had a situation when you meant well, however, your good ended up being evil spoken of or costly?

YOU CAN'T FLY WITH EAGLES

And Run With Turkeys

ISAIAH 40

That saying was often used by my late pastor Bishop Arthur M. Brazier when he tried to explain why those with great dreams had to separate themselves from those not going anywhere in life.

I am the oldest of seven siblings. My youngest brothers, who were twins, both suffered from Bipolar Disorder and were 19 years younger than me. On a personal note, I was very angry with my parents because my best friend at the time, was having his first child when the twins were born (and yes, they did have birth control then). My brothers both began using drugs and alcohol at very young ages and my mother wondered why they did not hang out with their achieving friends like now Senior Pastor Isaac B. Greene, a founding member of Victory Apostolic Church.

I told my Mom that my brothers only wanted to hang out with other "turkeys" like themselves, because the other turkeys never challenged them to fly and become more than what they were in spite of their mental illness.

It is the Prophet Isaiah who encourages young people and believers to fly with eagles (vv. 28-31).

SAC

It has been said that if you know a person's three closest friends, it will tell you that person's character. Are your three closest friends, eagles or turkeys in how they impact your life?

STOP STRESSING AND START ADAPTING

1 PETER 5

The above saying is another quote from Mr. Mike Lewis, a retired bank executive.

During the Pandemic, many businesses suffered greatly, especially restaurants and those in the hospitality industry. As businesses closed, the owners and staff incurred great financial stresses, even though some received economic stimulus packages.

Other businesses started adapting in a multiplicity of ways, such as finding ways to sell their products online, outside seating, carry outs, remote workplaces, etc.

It is true that necessity is the mother of invention. The Bible says believers are to cast all our cares and anxiety on God for he cares and will make a way (vs.7).

SAC

In what way did you or your business adapt in order to survive during the Pandemic?

IN THE MULTITUDE OF COUNSELORS

There is Safety

PROVERBS 15

It is impossible to be a leader either in the business or spiritual world without being faced with incredible, life-affecting decisions that have to be made. Some leaders surround themselves with "yes people" who tell them what they want to hear. That is not the case for me. I always seek out the advice of others who sometimes tell me exactly what I do not want to hear (Proverbs 15: 22) and two such examples are:

1. **My Mother's Advice**

   When I was 38 years old, I was called to the pastorate but waited until the age of 45 when I was led by the Holy Spirit to be the founding pastor of Victory. At 38, my mother said "It was far more important at that time, for me to be a father to my three young children." I am glad I took her advice because all of our children have made my wife and I proud because we put them first and made them our priority, which may not have happened with my increased responsibilities as a pastor.

2. **My Best Friend's Advice**

   During a time of great financial difficulty in the early years in our current church facility, I sought counsel from Mr. Rod Clemons, my best friend. As always, when I asked for his advice, he said, and I quote "You can do what you want to do, but this is what I think you should do." You see, the blessing of being a pastor is I can do whatever I want to do. The curse of being a pastor is I can do whatever I want to do. His advice forced me into a position of needing to have great humility, but I did it and God blessed that approach in resolving my financial problem at that time.

Remember the Bible says "pride comes before destruction and a haughty look before a fall" (Proverbs 16: 18).

SAC

Identify instances when not taking godly advice has caused bad consequences for you or those you love or serve.

I WISH THEM WELL

JOHN 13

I have learned that having the right attitude is key to handling the times when people leave Victory Apostolic Church. No pastor wants to lose members, just like no business man or woman wants to lose customers.

One day I asked my barber, Mr. Charles Freeman how he handled the loss of so many customers when he was forced to relocate his business. Without hesitation he replied "I wish them well." Immediately, the Holy Spirit enlightened me on how to properly handle members leaving my church; that is to wish them well. I now understand that people have a right to choose where they worship or do business. The spirit of genuine love and concern for others should always be that they will do well (vv. 34-35).

SAC

When have you felt bitterness, resentment, or abandonment by others due to a bad attitude?

BETTER A POOR MAN WITH INTEGRITY

Than A Rich Man Who is Crooked

PROVERBS 28

In 2021, Bernie Madoff died. Infamous for a Ponzi scheme that defrauded investors, many of them retirees, of billions of dollars, he died in a prison cell penniless.

How a person acquires their wealth is important because true riches are those that are character related. Proverbs 22:1 states "A good name is more desirable than great riches; to be esteemed is better than silver or gold."

I believe one of the greatest blessings a person can have is a good name and it is impossible to have a good name without being a person of integrity (Proverb 28:6).

SAC

As a part of being a light to the world, Christians must have integrity and live their lives above reproach to those who do not know God. Do your family and friends view you as a person of integrity? How do you maintain your integrity?

THE FOOLISHNESS OF HOLDING ON

To What You Can't Keep

LUKE 18

We live in the time of the billionaires around the world. People such as Jeff Bezos (Amazon), Oprah Winfrey, Bill Gates and many others have unimaginable wealth.

In Luke 18:18-30, Jesus encounters a rich young ruler who wants to know how to receive eternal life. When Jesus tells him to sell his fortune, give it to the poor and have treasure in heaven, he went away sorrowful. Jesus makes it clear that material riches can keep a person from entering the kingdom of God because money is their god (vv. 24-25).

The only man God calls a fool in Luke 12:20 did not understand that riches are temporary, and only what you do for God lasts. The Bible is clear that the believer is to store up treasure in heaven (Matthew 6:19-21).

SAC

If you have financial resources, one way to ensure that money is not your god is that you give to the poor and needy and your local church where you are fed spiritually (1 Timothy 6:17-19). Do you give to others in need?

YOU CAN BECOME WHATEVER YOU WANT TO BE

(With The Gifts God Gave You)

1 CORINTHIANS 7

I have often heard people say you can become whatever you want to be, but that's not true. Becoming what you want to be or do operates within the gifts God gave you. For instance, God has given me the gifts of preaching, teaching, and administration. I do not however, have the gifts of working with my hands in such fields as carpentry, electrical and construction, etc. Tools such as hammers, screwdrivers and drills become lethal weapons in my clumsy hands.

As Israel built the Tabernacle in the wilderness, he gave gifts to Bezalez and Oholiab to construct it (Exodus 35:30-36:1). God always equips people with the gifts necessary to carry out his purpose.

SAC

What are the gifts God has given you to serve Him and are you using them to build his kingdom on earth?

10 PERSONAL TRUTHS

IF YOU WANT TO STOP SEXUAL SINS

Follow The T.O.P. Principle

1 CORINTHIANS 6

Without a doubt this is my most quoted saying by members of Victory. As soon as I ask what is the T.O.P. Principle, the congregation responds:

T = Time

O = Opportunity

P = Place

It may sound simple, but it works. When you know you have sexual attractions that are wrong, whether you are single or married; not allowing time, opportunity and place to come together will keep you from committing sin. The Bible teaches us to stand against tests and trials with the whole armor of God, but when it comes to sexual temptation, the Bible says to run (for your life) (vv. 18-20).

It was the movie star Clint Eastwood who said in the film *Magnum Force* "A man (woman) must know his limitations." As believers our bodies are the temple of the Holy Spirit and our bodies should honor the Holy God who lives within us. Once lusts are allowed to grow in the mind, then you are not far from committing the physical act that will bring conviction and judgment from the Holy Spirit (Matthew 5:27-28; James 1:13-15).

SAC

How do you keep ungodly sexual attractions under control?

IF YOU DATE BAD, YOU MARRY BAD

2 CORINTHIANS 6

I. Ignoring the Obvious to Your Own Detriment

Before we get started, I know there will be some of you who are thinking, "Yes, I dated bad, but I married good." Congratulations! You are the exception to the rule.

You see, dating bad means that you ignore obvious personality and character flaws in a person, while believing that after getting married they will get corrected. However, the reality is that is that personality and character flaws tend to get worse under the lens of the 24-hour microscope called marriage.

II. Date Bad

I know that there are Christians who do not believe in dating. In our society, it is the way of getting to know someone better prior to marriage. Though the Bible says much about marriage, it says very little about how to identify the one that you are to "stick with forever" (Genesis 2: 21-25). The Old Testament also gives us obviously arranged marriages like the one between Isaac and Rebekah who seemed to be in love at first sight (Genesis 24: 57-67). It is the New Testament that teaches "what God has joined together, let no man put asunder" (Matthew 19:4-6). But how do we know if God joined a couple together?

I am listing three important tests and questions while you are dating that can guide you in determining if he/she is the right one for you.

SAC

1) *Are you compatible with each other? The Bible says don't be "unequally yoked." This applies to marriage, a person's faith, business, friends, etc., (2 Corinthians 6:14-18).*

2) *Does either party have an anger management issue? (Proverbs 14:17, 29; 15:1)*

3) *What does your family and close friends say about the person? Remember love may have you so blinded that you cannot see what is obvious to everyone else (Proverbs 15:22).*

MISERY, THE THING WORSE THAN LONELINESS

PROVERBS 17

I have counseled many times in situations where people are lonely. Some are single, never married, others divorced or widowed. Their loneliness is real, which is one of many things the Covid-19 Pandemic taught us when out of caution, physical contact with others became very limited.

I believe misery is worse than loneliness, especially in bad marriages where there are constant conflicts. Loneliness at least only involves one person (you); but misery is often due to the negative effect of others on your life.

Verse 1 of our text teaches that a meager amount of food (dry crust) with peace and quiet is better than a banquet where there is much arguing.

SAC

If you are dealing with loneliness, how has Jesus helped you by being the friend that sticks closer than a brother (John 15: 13-17).

INSEPARABLE LOVE

HEBREWS 13

This message was preached around Sweetest Day in October 2020. I know some of you get "sweet nothings" on that day, but for others, it is another day other than Valentine's Day to express love for a spouse, family member, friend, etc. The problem with all human relationships is that no matter how hard we try to keep them; they all are temporal. They all have a beginning and an end.

Since so few of our homes are two parent (husband and wife), it is important for wives with good husbands to show them how much they are appreciated. If you don't, some other woman will. You see, good husbands are like "TV dinners" which have been prepared elsewhere, but the person purchasing the dinner gets to enjoy it.

To you good husbands, do not forget your good wife is a gift from God, so treat her as such. As great as a marriage or friendship may be, only your relationship with God gives inseparable love. That love will be with you always in this world and the world to come (vs. 5; Romans 8:35-39).

SAC

What are you going to do to improve either your marriage or relationship with a friend that will make them feel appreciated and valued?

WITNESSING BEGINS IN THE HOME

ACTS 1

The book of Acts gives us among many other things the birth of the Jewish church and the spread of the gospel from Jerusalem to the uttermost parts of the earth. Jerusalem was home to the Jews (vs. 8). Our natural lives mirror our spiritual lives when the teaching of the gospel message begins at home. Victory's Mission of "Building Victorious Christlike Lives" begins with Christian values being first taught in the home.

When you do the simple thing of you and your family's life revolving around Christ, then the more complex thing of building a village or community is being built at the same time. I've used as a simple sermon illustration a four-piece puzzle with animals and when you turn it over, you see a complex whole zoo. That is what I mean when I say that when you build the simple you are simultaneously building the complex.

SAC

To build your life around Christ, every human being needs three homes (domestic, church, and eternal). Do you have all three homes? If so, are you witnessing to those who do not have all three homes.

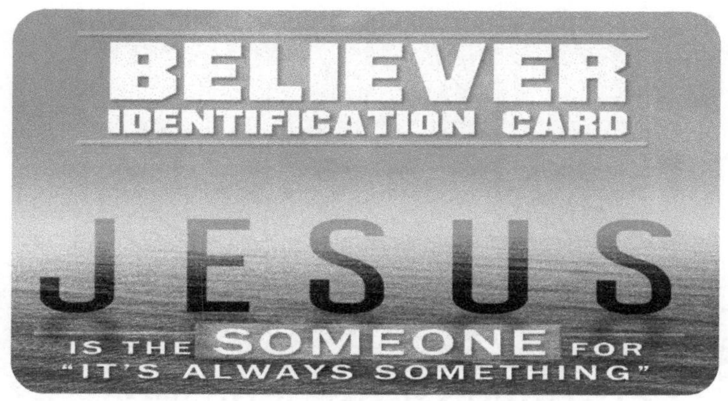

JESUS IS THE SOMEONE FOR WHEN

It Is Always Something

JOB 1

The Book of Job tells the story of a devout man named Job, whom Satan said to God that the only reason Job serves God is because of God's blessings; and that if God took them away Job would curse God. Satan was saying that Job put created things before the Creator of all things which is idolatry. There is nothing worse than someone who wants what you have, but they don't want you!

Job goes through tests to prove his fidelity to God based on who he is, not what he gives. Most of you can identify the times in life when one bad thing after another occurred. Job loses his wealth, servants, children and eventually his health. Job's faith identifies him as a believer as he retains his faith in God (vv.12-22). As believers today, we empathize with Job and know that "Jesus Is the Someone for It's Always Something."

SAC

When things are constantly going wrong in your life, do you blame God or praise God? Your praise of God in difficult times is your Believer's Identification Card.

A REAL FRIEND IS ONE WHO WALKS IN

When the Rest of the World Walks Out

MARK 2

Nothing proves friendship more than people helping you when you cannot help yourself.

The second chapter of Mark tells the story of a paralyzed man being carried to Jesus for healing by four men.

So many people were in the house where Jesus was teaching that there was no way to get their friend to Jesus. Their persistence shows when they made an opening in the roof of the house and lowered the paralyzed man to Jesus, he received both forgiveness of sins and physical healing (vv.1-12).

I am sure there are many untold stories during the Pandemic of those who would not have made it without their family and friends going beyond the call of duty.

SAC

Identify at least two people who either befriended you, or you befriended them during the Pandemic.

IF YOU HAVE MORE WISDOM

(YOU'LL NEED LESS FAITH)

JAMES 1

James, the Lord's half-brother, states that believers should understand the spiritual benefit of persevering through tests and trials, and the roles they play in becoming spiritually mature. But in verse 5, he connects faith to wisdom "if any of you lacks wisdom, you should ask God, who forgives generously to all without finding fault." James is talking about the wisdom it takes to endure test and trials.

Wisdom can also keep the believer from doing things that later requires faith. As an example, a person eats unhealthy, rarely exercises, stays under unbearable loads of stress, and the next thing you know they suffer a heart attack, stroke, etc. That person now goes to their pastor and says they have the faith to believe God for their healing (which He can do). However, if the person had the wisdom to take better care of themselves, they would never have had to experience the health issue.

The mother of one of Victory's pastors would say to him "Son, only a fool has to experience everything, and son, you are a fool" (Proverbs 3:13-18).

SAC

Identify two bad situations in your life that was caused by a lack of wisdom and good judgment on your part.

IT'S THE LIFE YOU CHOSE

PHILIPPIANS 2

I have only had two barbers since I was 12 years old and the second one, Charles Freeman has been my barber for over 30 years. Most men go to the barber for a haircut and shave, but in addition to those personal things being done, my barber has acted as a counselor to me.

One day I came into his shop feeling down after another draining day in a mega church environment. Charles asked "Had a rough day Reverend?" I replied, "yes" thinking he would be sympathetic. His response (I truly believe it was the Holy Spirit), "It's the life you chose."

No one made me become a pastor, it was God's call on my life, but I wanted and had accepted it. Just because what you are called to do gets hard at times, always remember "it is the life you chose" so put a smile on your face and be determined in your heart to complete God's purposes in your life (vv. 13-15).

SAC

What is your "it's the life you chose acceptance? Some of our greatest joys can bring the greatest pain; (career choice, marriage, family).

CONCLUDING TRUTH

MY TIMES ARE IN GOD'S HANDS

MY TIMES ARE IN GOD'S HANDS

ECCLESIASTES 3

On March 10, 2021, God blessed me to see my 70th birthday. King Solomon, the author of Ecclesiastes, says there are seasons and appointed times for everything under the sun, but we all start in the same place … birth. I can now say as King David did in Psalm 37:25, "I was young but now I'm old." It is only by God's grace and purposes for my life that I've made it this far. I don't feel old and I believe God has not finished his purpose for my life. You see, if you are not dead, you are not through (Psalm 92:12-15).

The various wheels of a clock work together to move the clocks hands forward. Behind the scenes, someway, somehow, God has worked everything together for my good and His glory (Romans 8:28).

As I age, I am clear life and death are but one thread. We don't choose the time we are born into, but we are accountable to God for what we do in our time.

SAC

In between the time we are born and the time we die, we live. So what are you doing with your living?

ABOUT THE AUTHOR

Andrew D. Singleton, Jr. is the founder and Senior Pastor of Victory Apostolic Church in Matteson, Illinois. Victory started with 12 members in 1996 and is now a mega-church in the southwest suburbs of Chicago. Pastor Singleton was mentored by his pastor the late great Bishop Arthur M Brazier of the Apostolic Church of God in Chicago, Illinois. He has been married to his college sweetheart, Brenda, for 47 years. They have three children, who are all saved and married, and eight grandchildren.

Educationally, Pastor Singleton has a Bachelor of Science in Accounting and a Master of Divinity degree from McCormick Theological Seminary. He also is a Certified Public Accountant and has served as a Chief Financial Officer of several non-profit organizations.

Visit us at: VACMatteson.org

About the Publisher

Let *Life to Legacy* bring your story to literary life! We offer the following publishing services: manuscript development, editing, transcription services, ghost-writing, cover design, copyright services, ISBN assignment, worldwide distribution, and eBook conversion.

We make the publishing process easy. Throughout production, we keep the author informed every step of the way. Even if you do not have a manuscript, that's not a problem for us. We can ghost-write your book from audio recordings or legible handwritten documents. Whether print-on-demand or trade publishing, we have packages to meet your publishing needs. At *Life to Legacy*, we take the stress out of becoming a published author.

Unlike other *so-called* publishers, we do more than just print books. Our books and eBooks are distributed to book buyers, distributors, and online retailers throughout the world. This is real publishing! Call us today for a free quote.

Please visit our website
www.Life2Legacy.com

or call us
877-267-7477

Send email inquiries to
Life2Legacybooks@att.net

CPSIA information can be obtained
at www.ICGtesting.com
Printed in the USA
BVHW062203190122
626634BV00012B/230